FOOD LOVERS

INDIAN

FOOD LOVERS

INDIAN

RECIPES SELECTED BY JONNIE LÉGER

Trans
Atlantic
Press

All recipes serve four people,
unless otherwise indicated.

For best results when cooking the recipes in this book, buy fresh ingredients and follow the instructions carefully. Make sure that everything is properly cooked through before serving, particularly any meat and shellfish, and note that as a general rule vulnerable groups such as the very young, elderly people, pregnant women, convalescents and anyone suffering from an illness should avoid dishes that contain raw or lightly cooked eggs.

For all recipes, quantities are given in standard U.S. cups and imperial measures, followed by the metric equivalent. Follow one set or the other, but not a mixture of both because conversions may not be exact. Standard spoon and cup measurements are level and are based on the following:

1 tsp. = 5 ml, 1 tbsp. = 15 ml, 1 cup = 250 ml / 8 fl oz.

Note that Australian standard tablespoons are 20 ml, so Australian readers should use 3 tsp. in place of 1 tbsp. when measuring small quantities.

The electric oven temperatures in this book are given for conventional ovens with top and bottom heat. When using a fan oven, the temperature should be decreased by about 20–40°F / 10–20°C – check the oven manufacturer's instruction book for further guidance. The cooking times given should be used as an approximate guideline only.

CONTENTS

CREAMY BLACK BEAN SOUP

Ingredients

2 tbsp oil

1 onion, chopped

2 garlic cloves, crushed

Thumb-size piece fresh ginger, peeled and grated

1 tsp ground cumin

½ tsp ground curcuma (turmeric)

3½ cups / 800 ml vegetable broth (stock)

2 tbsp tomato paste (purée)

1lb 6 oz / 600 g canned black beans, drained and rinsed

Scant 1 cup / 200 ml light (single) cream

1 tbsp balsamic vinegar

4 tbsp yogurt, to garnish

Salt and pepper

Dill sprigs, to garnish

Method

Prep and cook time: 45 min

1. Heat the oil in a large pan, add the onion and garlic and fry until soft but not brown.

2. Add the ginger, cumin and curcuma (turmeric) and fry for 30 seconds then pour in the broth (stock).

3. Add the tomato paste (purée) and beans. Bring to a boil, season with salt and pepper, then turn down the heat and simmer for 30 minutes.

4. Take out half of the beans, purée the soup, then put the beans back into the soup. Stir in the cream, reheat the soup and add the vinegar. If the soup is too thick, stir in a little water.

5. Ladle into bowls, add a swirl of yogurt to each and garnish with dill.

RED LENTIL SOUP

Ingredients

4 tbsp clarified butter or oil

1 onion, finely sliced

2 garlic cloves

Thumb-size piece ginger, peeled and chopped

1 red chili pepper, deseeded and finely chopped

2 tsp curry powder

1 tsp curcuma (turmeric)

1½ cups / 300 g red lentils

1 cup / 200 g canned tomatoes, chopped

3 cups / 750 ml chicken broth (stock)

Salt and pepper

2 scallions (spring onions), sliced diagonally, to garnish

2 tbsp chopped cilantro (fresh coriander), to garnish

Method

Prep and cook time: 25 min

1. Heat the butter in a deep pan and fry the onions until soft but not brown.

2. Add the garlic, ginger, chili pepper, curry powder and curcuma (turmeric) and cook for 2 minutes then add the lentils and stir well.

3. Pour in the tomatoes and chicken broth (stock), season with salt and pepper and simmer very gently for about 20 minutes or until the lentils are tender.

4. Serve garnished with scallions (spring onions) and cilantro (fresh coriander).

CHICKEN SOUP WITH ALMONDS

Ingredients

4 tbsp sunflower oil

4 chicken breasts, skinned and cut into chunks

2 onions, finely chopped

3 garlic cloves, chopped

2 tsp ground cumin

½ tsp cayenne pepper

1 tsp each of: ground ginger, ground coriander and curcuma (turmeric)

²/₃ cup / 100 g ground almonds

2 cups / 500 ml chicken broth (stock)

Salt and pepper

½ cup / 125 ml yogurt

1 cup / 75 g flaked almonds

1 tsp saffron threads, to garnish

2 tbsp sesame seeds, lightly toasted in a dry pan, to garnish

Method

Prep and cook time: 45 min

1. Heat the oil in a wide pan and fry the chicken pieces for 5 minutes or until lightly browned all over. Remove from the pan and keep warm.

2. Gently fry the onions in the pan until softened but not brown then stir in the garlic and spices. Cook for 2 minutes, stirring all the time.

3. Add the ground almonds and chicken broth (stock), season with salt and pepper then add the chicken and simmer very gently for 20 minutes.

4. Spoon in the yogurt and flaked almonds and simmer very gently for 5 more minutes.

5. Serve the soup in warmed bowls with the saffron threads and sesame seeds sprinkled over.

LAMB SAMOSAS

Ingredients

For the dough:

3 cups / 300 g all-purpose (plain) flour

4 tbsp clarified butter

1 tsp salt

For the filling:

4 tbsp clarified butter

½ tsp ground ginger

½ tsp ground cumin

½ tsp ground coriander

½ tsp chili powder

1 tsp garam masala

1 onion, very finely chopped

1 lb / 450 g ground (minced) lamb

1¼ cups / 125 g frozen peas, thawed

1 tsp salt

Approx 2 pints / 1 liter vegetable oil, for frying

Method

Prep and cook time: 1 hour

1. For the dough, mix the flour, clarified butter and salt together with enough warm water to form a soft dough. Turn onto a floured board and knead for 3 minutes then return to the bowl and let rest while you make the filling.

2. For the filling, heat the clarified butter in a wide pan and gently fry the spices for 2 minutes.

3. Add the onion, cook until softened then stir in the lamb, peas and salt. Cook for about 5 minutes or until the meat is well browned then set aside.

4. Divide the dough into 8 pieces and roll each one out on a floured board to make a circle about 8 inches / 20 cm in diameter.

5. Cut each circle in half, place a little of the filling on one half of each semi-circle, moisten the edges with water then fold over the pastry and press together the edges to make a tight seal.

6. Heat the oil in a deep pan until small bubble rise to the surface then deep fry the samosas in batches for 3–4 minutes, turning once, until they are golden brown.

7. Drain the samosas on kitchen paper and serve warm.

Makes 16

PORK WITH GINGER AND CHILI

Ingredients

1½ lb / 800 g boned pork leg, trimmed of fat and cubed

3 tbsp vegetable oil

1 large onion, chopped

2 garlic cloves, finely chopped

1 red chili pepper, deseeded and finely sliced

Thumb-size piece fresh ginger, peeled and grated

½ tsp ground coriander

½ tsp ground curcuma (turmeric)

½ tsp ground cloves

½ tsp ground cumin

2 cups / 400 g canned tomatoes, chopped

2/3 cup / 150 ml yogurt

Salt and pepper

2 tbsp chopped parsley, to garnish

Method

Prep and cook time: 1 hour 10 min

1. Heat the oil in a skillet (frying pan) and sear the meat on all sides until golden brown. Remove the meat from the pan and keep warm.

2. Add the onions to the pan, cook until softened but not brown then stir in the garlic, chili, ginger, coriander, curcuma (turmeric), cloves and cumin.

3. Cook the spices for 2 minutes then return the meat to the pan with the tomatoes and yogurt.

4. Season with salt and pepper then bring to a simmer and cook very gently for about 45 minutes or until the meat is tender. Add a little water during cooking if the dish looks too dry.

5. Serve sprinked with the parsley.

ALOO BAINGAN

Ingredients

6 large potatoes, peeled and cut into chunks

½ cup / 125 ml vegetable oil

2 onions, finely chopped

2 garlic cloves, finely chopped

Thumb-size piece ginger, peeled and grated

2 tbsp fennel seeds

1 red chili pepper, deseeded and finely chopped

1 tsp curcuma (turmeric)

1 tsp ground coriander

1 tsp sugar

2 tbsp tomato paste (purée)

2 large eggplants (aubergines), diced

Salt and pepper

To garnish:

3 tbsp oil

1 red bell pepper, deseeded and sliced

1 tbsp chopped cilantro (coriander)

Method

Prep and cook time: 45 min

1. Boil the potatoes in salted water until just tender. Drain well and set aside.

2. Meanwhile, heat the oil in a wide pan and cook the onions very gently until soft but not brown.

3. Add the garlic, ginger, fennel seeds, chili, curcuma (turmeric) and coriander and cook for 2 minutes.

4. Stir in the sugar and tomato paste (purée) then add the eggplant (aubergine) and about a cup (250 ml) of water. Season with salt and pepper and simmer very gently, stirring from time to time, for 20 minutes or until the eggplant is very soft then mash with a fork.

5. Meanwhile, heat the oil for the garnish in a skillet and fry the bell peppers for 5 minutes. Remove from the skillet and set aside.

6. Add the cooked potatoes to the eggplant sauce, cook for 5 more minutes then serve garnished with the bell pepper and cilantro (coriander) leaves.

LAMB AND TOMATO CURRY

Ingredients

Thumb-size piece fresh ginger, peeled and chopped

1 tbsp garam masala

2 lbs / 900 g lean lamb, cut into large chunks

6 tbsp vegetable oil

4 onions, diced

2 garlic cloves, sliced

1 green chili pepper, deseeded and finely chopped

½ tsp ground cumin

1 tsp paprika

Salt and pepper

2 tbsp tomato paste (purée)

3 tomatoes, diced

8 sprigs cilantro (fresh coriander), leaves and stalks, finely chopped

4 tbsp yogurt

Method

Prep and cook time: 1 hour 20 min plus 30 min to marinate

1. Mix the ginger with the garam masala and rub into the lamb chunks. Marinate at room temperature for at least 30 minutes.

2. Heat 2 tbsp of oil in a large pan and fry the onion, garlic and chili pepper on a gentle heat until softened but not brown. Stir in the cumin and paprika and season with salt and pepper. Cook for 2 minutes then remove the mixture from the pan and set aside.

3. Heat the remaining oil in the pan and fry the lamb on a medium heat on all sides for 5 minutes.

4. Stir the tomato paste (purée) into the pan, add the onion mixture and pour over 3 cups / 750 ml water.

5. Bring to a boil then reduce the heat and cook very gently, stirring occasionally, for 1 hour or until the meat is tender.

6. Check the seasoning then divide between 4 bowls and garnish with the cilantro (coriander), diced tomatoes and yogurt.

LENTIL STEW

Ingredients

1 cup / 150 g cashew nuts

4 tbsp vegetable oil

½ cup / 100 g split red lentils, washed
and drained

½ tsp ground coriander

½ tsp ground cloves

½ tsp cumin

1 leek, sliced

1 carrot, cut into batons

1 potato, peeled and cut into chunks

2 cups / 500 ml vegetable broth (stock)

1 cup / 200 g canned chickpeas,
drained and rinsed

Salt and pepper

Cilantro leaves (fresh coriander),
to garnish

Method

Prep and cook time: 40 min

1. Roast the cashew nuts in a dry skillet until lightly browned then set aside.

2. Heat the oil in a large pan and stir in the lentils, coriander, cloves and cumin. Cook for 2 minutes then add the leek, carrot and potato.

3. Pour in the broth (stock) and chickpeas, season with salt and pepper and simmer gently for 20 minutes, stirring from time to time, or until the lentils are tender.

4. Add the cashew nuts, heat through and serve garnished with cilantro (coriander) leaves.

EGGPLANTS IN PEANUT SAUCE

Ingredients

6 tbsp oil

2 lb / 900 g baby eggplants (aubergines)

2 onions, chopped

2 garlic cloves, chopped

Thumb-size piece ginger, peeled and chopped

2 red chili peppers, deseeded and chopped

2 tsp coriander seeds

1 tsp cumin seeds

1 tsp mustard seeds

2 tbsp desiccated coconut

1 tbsp tamarind paste

3 tbsp tomato paste (purée)

Salt and pepper

12 green beans, halved

1¾ cups / 200 g peanuts, chopped

Method

Prep and cook time: 40 min

1. Heat the oil in a wide pan and gently cook the whole eggplants (aubergines) until tender. Do not allow them to brown.

2. Remove the eggplants from the pan and set half aside. Scoop the flesh from the other half and set aside.

3. Cook the onions very gently until soft but not brown then add the garlic, ginger, chili, coriander seeds, cumin seeds and mustard seeds and cook for 2 minutes.

4. Stir in the coconut, tamarind paste and tomato paste (purée) and cook for 2 minutes.

5. Add the chopped eggplant flesh and half a cup of water, season with salt and pepper and simmer very gently, stirring from time to time, for 20 minutes. Add a little more water during cooking if needed.

6. Meanwhile, blanch the beans in boiling salted water for 3 minutes and add to the pan.

7. Lightly toast the peanuts in a dry pan and add to the curry. Return the whole eggplants to the pan, heat though and serve.

COD CURRY WITH SPINACH

Ingredients

For the spinach:
3 tbsp oil
1 onion, finely chopped
2 garlic cloves, chopped
2 tsp garam masala
4 large handfuls spinach, washed and finely chopped
1 tbsp butter
Salt and pepper

For the cod curry:

3 tbsp oil

1 tsp chili powder

1 tsp curcuma (turmeric)

2 tsp garam masala

½ cup / 125 ml coconut milk

½ cup / 125 ml fish broth (stock)

1 lb 8 oz / 650 g cod, cut into chunks

Method
Prep and cook time: 40 min

1. For the spinach, heat the oil in wide pan and cook the onion until soft but not brown.

2. Add the garlic and garam masala and cook for 2 minutes then add the spinach and cook very gently, stirring from time to time, for 10 minutes. Stir in the butter, season with salt and pepper. Set aside and keep warm.

3. For the curry, heat the oil in a wide pan and fry the chili powder, curcuma (turmeric) and garam masala for 2 minutes.

4. Pour over the coconut milk and fish broth (stock), bring to a boil and simmer for 10 minutes. Season with salt and pepper, add the cod and cook very gently for 5 minutes or until the cod is just cooked through.

5. Serve with boiled rice.

KOFTA CURRY

Ingredients

For the sauce:

3 tbsp oil

1 onion, chopped

2 garlic cloves, chopped

Thumb-size piece ginger, finely chopped

1 tsp each of: curcuma (turmeric), chili powder, paprika, ground cinnamon and ground coriander

2 cups / 400 g canned tomatoes

1 cup / 250 ml vegetable broth (stock)

Salt and pepper

For the kofta:

1 onion, roughly chopped

2 garlic cloves, chopped

2 tbsp chopped cilantro (coriander)

2 tbsp chopped parsley

1 tsp ground cinnamon

1 lb / 450 g ground (minced) beef

1 egg, beaten

4 tbsp oil

For the batter:

4 eggs

½ cup / 50 g flour

1 tsp baking powder

1 tsp salt

Oil, for deep frying

To serve:

12 cherry tomatoes, quartered

Chopped parsley

Method
Prep and cook time: 1 hour

1. For the sauce, heat the oil in a deep pan and gently cook the onion until soft but not brown.

2. Add the garlic, ginger and all the spices and cook for 2 minutes, stirring all the time.

3. Pour in the tomatoes and vegetable broth (stock), season with salt and pepper and simmer gently for 15 minutes.

4. Blend the sauce to a purée, pass through a fine sieve and keep warm.

5. For the koftas, put the onion, garlic, cilantro (coriander), cinnamon and parsley in a food processor and blend to make a paste.

6. Mix the paste with the beef and beaten egg, season with salt and pepper and roll into balls.

7. Heat the oil in a skillet and fry the koftas for 5 minutes making sure they are evenly cooked.

8. Beat the batter ingredients together with half a cup of warm water. Heat the oil in a deep pan until bubbles appear on a wooden spoon held in the oil. Dip the koftas into the batter and deep fry in batches until golden brown. Drain on kitchen paper.

9. Serve the koftas in the sauce with the cherry tomatoes and parsley scattered over.

SPICED SPINACH WITH CHILI PEPPERS

Ingredients

3 tbsp clarified butter or oil

4 whole red chili peppers

1 onion, finely sliced

1 garlic clove, finely chopped

Thumb-size piece ginger, peeled and finely chopped

1 tsp coriander seeds

1 tsp cumin seeds

1 tsp black mustard seeds

1lb 12 oz / 750 g spinach, washed and roughly chopped

Salt and pepper

Method
Prep and cook time: 20 min

1. Heat the butter in a pan and gently fry the whole red chili peppers for 2 minutes or until just starting to soften. Remove from the pan and set aside.

2. Fry the sliced onion in the pan until soft but not brown then add the garlic, ginger, coriander seeds, cumin seeds and mustard seeds.

3. Cook very gently for 5 minutes then add the spinach. Cover with a lid and cook for 2 minutes or until the spinach is wilted and soft. Season with salt and pepper and serve garnished with the whole chili peppers.

SHRIMP CURRY

Ingredients

1 onion, roughly chopped

2 garlic cloves, chopped

Thumb-size piece ginger, peeled and chopped

1 red chili pepper, deseeded and chopped

3 tbsp clarified butter or oil

1 tsp salt

1 tsp paprika

1 tsp garam masala

½ tsp curcuma (turmeric)

2 tbsp tomato paste (purée)

2 cups / 500 ml coconut milk

1 cup / 250 ml fish broth (stock) or water

1 lb 8 oz / 650 g large shrimps, peeled with tail on

Salt and pepper

Cilantro (coriander) leaves, to garnish

Method

Prep and cook time: 30 min

1. Put the onion, garlic, ginger and chili pepper in a food processor and blend to make a purée.

2. Heat the butter in a wide pan and add the onion mixture. Cook for 1 minute then add the salt, paprika, garam masala and curcuma (turmeric) and cook for 2 minutes, stirring all the time.

3. Stir in the tomato paste (purée) then pour in the coconut milk and fish broth (stock). Bring to a boil then simmer gently for 10 minutes.

4. Add the shrimps, season with salt and pepper and cook for a few minutes. Serve garnished with cilantro (coriander) and accompanied with boiled rice.

MONKFISH IN BANANA LEAVES

Ingredients

4 large banana leaves

2 tbsp oil

1 onion, roughly chopped

2 green chili peppers, deseeded and roughly chopped

Thumb-size piece ginger, peeled and roughly chopped

1 stick lemongrass, roughly chopped

1 garlic clove, roughly chopped

1 handful cilantro (coriander) leaves

Zest and juice of 2 limes

1 cup / 250 ml coconut milk

1 tsp fish sauce

1 tsp sugar

4 pieces monkfish fillet, approx
8 oz / 225 g each, skin on

1 lime, cut into wedges, to garnish

Method
Prep and cook time: 35 min

1. Heat the oven to 425°F (220°C / Gas Mark 7).

2. Soften the banana leaves by carefully holding over a gas flame then set aside.

3. Put all the ingredients apart from the monkfish into a food processor and pulse to make a coarse paste.

4. Slice the skin away from the flesh of the monkfish, leaving a hinge at one end. Place a piece of fish skin side down on each banana leaf, spoon the paste under the skin and wrap up the banana leaf. Secure with kitchen twine.

5. Place the stuffed banana leaves on a cookie sheet and bake in the oven for 20 minutes. Serve with lime wedges.

CHICKEN WITH ALMONDS

Ingredients

3 tbsp clarified butter or oil

1 onion, finely chopped

2 garlic cloves, finely sliced

1 tsp curcuma (turmeric)

4 chicken breasts, skinned and
cut into chunks

½ cup / 125 ml chicken broth (stock)

½ cup / 125 ml heavy (double) cream

⅓ cup / 50 g ground almonds

4 pieces cinnamon

⅔ cup / 50 g flaked almonds,
lightly toasted

2 tbsp chopped parsley

2 tbsp chopped cilantro (coriander)
plus some to garnish

Salt and pepper

1 tsp paprika

Method
Prep and cook time: 30 min

1. Heat the butter in a large pan and gently fry the onion and garlic until soft.

2. Stir in the curcuma (turmeric), cook for 2 minutes then add the chicken and stir briefly. Pour over the chicken broth (stock) and cream and stir in the ground almonds and cinnamon.

3. Simmer very gently, stirring from time to time, for about 20 minutes or until the chicken is cooked through.

4. Stir in the flaked almonds and chopped herbs, season with salt and pepper and serve with the paprika sprinkled over and the cilantro (coriander) to garnish.

SPICED LAMB WITH CHICKPEAS

Ingredients

3 tbsp clarified butter or oil

1 lb 8 oz / 600 g lamb, from the leg, cubed

1 onion, finely chopped

2 garlic cloves, chopped

1 red chili pepper, deseeded and finely chopped

2 tsp garam masala

1 tsp ground coriander

1 tsp cumin

4 medium potatoes, peeled and cut into chunks

2 cups / 400 g canned tomatoes, chopped

½ cup / 125 ml lamb broth (stock) or water

2 cups / 400 g canned chickpeas, drained and rinsed

Salt and pepper

Method

Prep and cook time: 1 hour

1. Heat the butter in a deep pan and gently fry the lamb until browned all over.

2. Add the onion, garlic, chili pepper, garam masala, coriander and cumin and cook for 2 minutes.

3. Add the potatoes, stir for 1 minute then add the tomatoes and the lamb broth (stock). Season with salt and pepper and simmer very gently for 30 minutes. Add more water during cooking if needed.

4. Add the chickpeas and cook for 15 minutes more or until the lamb is very tender.

WHITE CABBAGE CURRY

Ingredients

3 tbsp clarified butter or oil

Thumb-size piece ginger, peeled and grated

2 tsp garam masala

1 tsp ground coriander

1 tsp curcuma (turmeric)

1 tsp ground cumin

2 bay leaves

1 small white cabbage, trimmed and shredded

1 lb / 450 g waxy potatoes, peeled and cubed

Salt and pepper

1 cup / 150 g frozen peas

2 large tomatoes, deseeded and diced

Method

Prep and cook time: 25 min

1. Heat the clarified butter or oil in a large skillet and gently fry the ginger, garam masala, coriander, curcuma (turmeric), cumin and bay leaves for 3 minutes, stirring all the time.

2. Stir in the cabbage and the potatoes, cook for 2 minutes then add about ½ cup (125 ml) of water. Season with salt and pepper and cook for 10 minutes, stirring from time to time. Add more water if needed.

3. Add the peas and tomatoes, cook for 5 more minutes then serve accompanied with rice.

BEEF VINDALOO

Ingredients

3 tbsp clarified butter or oil

1 lb / 450 g braising beef,
cut into chunks

2 onions, finely chopped

2 garlic cloves, chopped

2 red chili peppers, deseeded
and chopped

1 tsp each of: cumin seeds, mustard
seeds, curcuma (turmeric) and paprika

2 tsp ground coriander

2 tsp garam masala

½ tsp dried chili flakes (optional)

2 tbsp tomato paste (purée)

2 cups / 400 g canned tomatoes,
chopped

⅓ cup / 75 ml white wine vinegar

2 cups / 500 ml beef broth (stock)

Salt and pepper

Mint leaves, to garnish

Poppadoms, to serve

Method
Prep and cook time: 1 hour 15 min

1. Heat the butter in a large pan and gently fry the pieces of meat in batches until they are brown all over. Remove from the pan and set aside.

2. Fry the onions in the pan until soft but not brown then add the garlic, chili peppers and all the spices. Cook for 2 minutes then stir in the tomato paste (purée).

3. Return the meat to the pan, cook for about a minute then add the canned tomatoes, vinegar and beef broth (stock). Season with salt and pepper and simmer very gently for about 45 minutes or until the meat is very tender.

4. Serve the curry garnished with mint leaves and poppadoms alongside.

LAMB ROGAN JOSH

Ingredients

6 tbsp vegetable oil

2¼ lbs / 1kg lamb, cut into large chunks

1 onion, chopped

4 garlic cloves, chopped

Thumb-size piece fresh ginger, peeled and chopped

1 tsp ground cinnamon

2 tsp ground cumin

2 tsp ground coriander

1 tsp chili powder

2 tbsp tomato paste (purée)

2 cups / 400 g canned tomatoes, chopped

Salt and pepper

Cilantro (fresh coriander), to garnish

Method

Prep and cook time: 1 hour 30 min

1. Heat 4 tbsp of the oil in a large pan and fry the lamb pieces until browned all over. Remove the meat from the pan and set aside.

2. Heat the remaining oil in the pan and gently cook the onion until softened. Add the garlic and the spices and cook for 2 minutes.

3. Stir in the tomato paste (purée) and return the meat to the pan. Add the canned tomatoes, season with salt and pepper and cook very gently, stirring from time to time, for about 1¼ hours or until the meat is very tender. You might need to add a little water during cooking to prevent the sauce from becoming too dry. Serve garnished with cilantro (fresh coriander).

SALMON CURRY WITH MANGO

Ingredients

3 tbsp clarified butter or oil

1 onion, very finely chopped

2 garlic cloves, finely chopped

½ tsp curcuma (turmeric)

Thumb-size piece ginger, peeled and finely chopped

1 green chili pepper, deseeded and finely chopped

3 cups / 750 ml fish broth (stock)

Juice of 2 limes

1 lb 8 oz / 650 g salmon fillet, skinned and cut into chunks

2 mangoes, peeled, stones removed and cut into chunks

1 cup / 100 g desiccated coconut

2 tbsp chopped cilantro (fresh coriander) plus some to garnish

2 tbsp black mustard seeds, lightly toasted

Method

Prep and cook time: 30 min

1. Heat the butter in a wide pan and gently fry the onion until soft but not brown.

2. Add the garlic, curcuma (turmeric), ginger and chili pepper and cook for 2 more minutes then add the fish broth (stock) and lime juice.

3. Bring to a boil then turn the heat down and add the salmon, mango and coconut. Simmer for 10 minutes or until the salmon is cooked through, then stir in the chopped cilantro (coriander).

4. Serve with the mustard seeds scattered over and garnish with cilantro sprigs.

MANGO CHICKEN

Ingredients

4 tbsp clarified butter or oil

4 chicken thighs, cut in half through the bone

4 onions, sliced

2 garlic cloves, crushed

Thumb-size piece fresh ginger, peeled and grated

1 tsp curcuma (turmeric)

1 tsp paprika

1 tsp ground cumin

1 tsp ground coriander

1 cup / 250 ml chicken broth (stock)

1 cup / 250 ml coconut milk

1 cup / 200 g mango chutney

Juice of 1 lemon

Salt and pepper

1 red chili pepper, deseeded and finely sliced

Method

Prep and cook time: 50 min

1. Heat the butter in a wide pan and cook the chicken pieces until lightly browned all over. Remove from the pan and set aside.

2. Gently fry the onions until soft but not brown then add the garlic, ginger, curcuma (turmeric), paprika, cumin and coriander. Fry for 2 minutes, stirring all the time.

3. Return the chicken to the pan, stir to coat in the spices then pour in the chicken broth (stock) and coconut milk. Simmer gently for 20 minutes then add the mango chutney and lemon juice and season with salt and pepper.

4. Let simmer for another 15 minutes or until the chicken is cooked through. Serve with the sliced chili scattered over.

BUTTER CHICKEN

Ingredients

½ cup / 125 ml yogurt

3 tbsp ground almonds

2–3 tsp garam masala

1 pinch Indian five-spice powder

1 pinch cinnamon

1 cardamom pod, crushed

1 tsp ground ginger

2 garlic cloves, crushed

1 cup / 200 g canned tomatoes, chopped

1 tsp salt

4 medium chicken breasts, skinned and chopped into bite-size chunks

3 tbsp clarified butter or oil

1 onion, finely chopped

½ cup / 125 ml coconut milk

½ cup / 125 ml vegetable broth (stock) or water

2 handfuls spinach, washed

Salt and pepper

Method

Prep and cook time: 40 min plus
3 hours to marinate

1. Mix the yogurt, ground almonds, garam masala, five-spice, cinnamon, cardamom, ginger, garlic, tomatoes and salt.

2. Put the chicken into a large bowl and pour the yogurt sauce over it. Mix and leave to stand in a cool place for at least 3 hours.

3. Heat the butter in a deep skillet, add the onion and cook for 5 minutes.

4. Add the chicken and yogurt mixture, coconut milk and vegetable broth (stock). Bring to a boil then simmer over a low heat for 20 minutes or until the chicken is cooked through and the sauce has thickened.

5. Stir in the spinach and cook very gently for 5 minutes. Season to taste with salt and serve.

CHICKEN KORMA

Ingredients

3 tbsp clarified butter or oil

1 onion, finely chopped

Thumb-size piece ginger, peeled and grated

2 garlic cloves, chopped

2 cloves, crushed

1 dried chili pepper, crushed

2 cardamom pods, crushed

1 tsp ground cumin

4 chicken breasts, skinned and cut into chunks

½ cup / 75 g ground almonds

1 cup / 250 ml chicken broth (stock)

½ cup / 125 ml heavy (double) cream

Salt and pepper

1 tbsp chopped cilantro (coriander) leaves

Method

Prep and cook time: 30 min

1. Heat the clarified butter in a large skillet and gently fry the onion, ginger and garlic until soft.

2. Stir in the crushed cloves, chili, cardamom and cumin and cook for 2 minutes, stirring all the time.

3. Add the chicken, brown the meat on all sides then stir in the almonds, chicken broth (stock) and cream. Simmer very gently for about 20 minutes or until the chicken is cooked through and the sauce is thick and creamy. Season to taste with salt and pepper.

4. Serve the korma with the rice and scatter over the cilantro (coriander).

SEA BASS WITH INDIAN SPICES

Ingredients

2 tbsp clarified butter or oil

2 onions, chopped

1 red chili pepper, deseeded and finely chopped

1 tsp curcuma (turmeric)

1 tbsp garam masala

1 tbsp red curry paste

2 tomatoes, roughly chopped

3 tbsp lime juice, plus extra to taste

½ cup / 125 ml coconut milk

2 cups / 500 ml fish or vegetable broth (stock)

4 sea bass steaks

Cilantro (fresh coriander), chopped

Salt and pepper

Method

Prep and cook time: 45 min

1. Heat the butter in a deep skillet and fry the onions on a medium heat for 3–4 minutes.

2. Add the chili pepper, curcuma (turmeric), garam masala, red curry paste and tomatoes and fry together for 1 minute. Stir in the lime juice, coconut milk and broth (stock). Simmer for 5–8 minutes with a lid on.

3. Add the fish to the sauce and cook on a low heat for 7–10 minutes. The fish is cooked when the flesh comes away from the bone.

4. Just before serving stir the cilantro (coriander) into the sauce. Season with salt, pepper and the remaining lime juice.

CHICKEN SKEWERS WITH RAITA

Ingredients

For the skewers:

1 garlic clove, finely chopped

2 tsp curcuma (turmeric)

1 tsp curry powder

2 tbsp oil

Juice of ½ lime

4 chicken breasts, skinned and cut into chunks

For the raita:

1 cup / 250 ml yogurt

½ cucumber, deseeded and chopped

2 mint sprigs, leaves chopped

1 green chili pepper, chopped

1 tsp salt

Lime wedges, to garnish

Method

Prep and cook time: 20 min plus
2 hours marinating time

1. Mix together the garlic, curcuma (turmeric), curry powder, oil and lime juice. Mix in the chicken chunks and leave to marinate for 2 hours.

2. For the raita, mix togther all the ingredients and set aside.

3. Heat the broiler (grill) to a medium setting. Thread the chicken onto wooden skewers and broil (grill) for about 6 minutes, turning from time to time, or until the chicken is cooked through.

4. Serve the kebabs with the raita and garnish with lime wedges.

BAINGAN BEMISAL

Ingredients

6 small eggplants (aubergines), sliced in half lengthways

6 tbsp vegetable oil

2 onions, chopped

2 garlic cloves, crushed

Thumb-size piece ginger, peeled and finely chopped

1 tsp curcuma (turmeric)

1 tsp ground coriander

1 tsp ground cumin

1 tsp garam masala

1 red bell pepper, deseeded and cut into chunks

1 potato, peeled, cut into chunks

Salt and pepper

Sesame seeds, to serve

Method

Prep and cook time: 35 min

1. Heat the oven to 375°F, (180°C / Gas Mark 5).

2. Brush the eggplant (aubergine) skins and flesh with a little of the oil and place in a roasting pan. Cover with kitchen foil and bake for about 20 minutes or until the flesh is tender.

3. While the eggplants are cooking, boil the potato in salted water until just tender and heat the remaining oil in a wide pan and gently cook the onion and garlic until soft but not brown.

4. Add the ginger, curcuma (turmeric), coriander, cumin and garam masala then cook for 2 minutes. Stir in the bell peppers and cooked potato.

5. Cook very gently, stirring from time to time, for 6 minutes or until the bell pepper is tender.

6. Remove the eggplants from the oven and scoop out the flesh from the centers, leaving a wall about ½ inch / 1 cm thick.

7. Roughly chop the eggplant flesh and stir into the onion/spice mixture. Season with salt and pepper and spoon into the hollowed out eggplants.

8. Scatter over the sesame seeds and serve immediately.

GROUND LAMB, POTATO AND SPINACH CURRY

Ingredients

5 tbsp clarified butter or oil

2 garlic cloves, finely chopped

2 tsp garam masala

1 tsp ground coriander

1 tsp ground cumin

1 lb / 450 g ground (minced) lamb

Salt and pepper

2 onions, sliced

Thumb-size piece ginger, finely chopped

1 red chili pepper, deseeded and finely chopped

1 tsp curcuma (turmeric)

6 large potatoes, peeled and cut into chunks

2 cups / 500 ml meat broth (stock)

1 cup / 250 ml yogurt

2 large handfuls spinach, washed and roughly chopped

Method

Prep and cook time: 1 hour

1. Heat 3 tbsp of the butter in a wide pan and fry the garlic, garam masala, coriander and cumin for 2 minutes.

2. Add the lamb and fry for 5 minutes or until the lamb is browned all over then pour in about a cup (250 ml) of water and cook with a lid on for about 15 minutes, stirring from time to time. Remove the lid, cook until the water has evaporated then season with salt and pepper and set aside.

3. Heat the remaining butter a clean pan and gently fry the onions for 2 minutes. Add the ginger, chili pepper and curcuma (turmeric) and cook for 2 more minutes.

4. Add the potatoes, stir for 2 minutes to coat the potatoes with the spices then pour in the meat broth (stock). Bring to a boil then turn the heat down and add the yogurt. Season with salt and pepper and simmer very gently for 15 minutes or until the potatoes are tender.

5. Wilt the spinach in a pan with a splash of water then drain and squeeze out the excess moisture.

6. To serve, place the cooked lamb onto warmed serving dishes, top with the spinach and pour over the onion and potato mixture.

BEEF BIRYANI
WITH FRIED ONIONS

Ingredients

½ cup /125 ml clarified butter or oil

2 onions, finely sliced

2 onions, roughly chopped

2 thumb-size pieces ginger, peeled and roughly chopped

3 garlic cloves, roughly chopped

2 green chili peppers, deseeded and roughly chopped

4 cloves

4 cardamom pods

1 tsp garam masala

1 tsp ground cinnamon

Juice of 2 limes

2 lb / 900 g beef, cut into large chunks

1 cup / 200 g long grain rice

6 strands saffron

Salt and pepper

Mint leaves, to garnish

Method

Prep and cook time: 1 hour 20 min
plus 1 hour marinating

1. Put the chopped onions, ginger, garlic, chili peppers, the spices and lime juice in a food processor and blend briefly to make a coarse purée.

2. Rub the onion purée into the beef and set aside to marinate for 1 hour.

3. Heat the butter in a deep pan and fry the sliced onions until brown and crisp. Remove from the pan, drain on kitchen paper and set aside.

4. Heat the pan with the butter used to cook the sliced onions and add the beef and the marinade. Fry until the meat is browned on all sides then add about 1 cup of water, salt and pepper and simmer very, very gently with a lid on for about 1 hour or until the meat is very tender. Add a little more water during the cooking if needed to prevent the dish burning.

5. While the meat is cooking, prepare the rice according to the packet instructions. Dissolve the saffron strands in a little hot water and stir into half the rice. Mix the saffron rice into the white rice.

6. Serve the meat and its sauce with the rice, scatter over the fried onions and garnish with mint leaves.

LAMB SAAG

Ingredients

1 onion, roughly chopped

3 garlic cloves

Thumb-size piece ginger, peeled and roughly chopped

2 green chili peppers, deseeded and roughly chopped

½ cup / 125 ml vegetable oil

2 lbs / 900 g lamb shoulder, cut into large chunks

2 tsp coriander seeds, crushed

2 cardamom pods, crushed

1 tsp cumin seeds, crushed

1 tsp garam masala

1 tsp curcuma (turmeric)

1 tsp salt

1 tbsp tomato paste (purée)

1 cup / 250 ml lamb broth (stock) or water

2 large handfuls spinach, washed and roughly chopped

Method

Prep and cook time: 1 hour 30 min

1. Put the onion, garlic, ginger and chili peppers in a food processor and blend to make a purée.

2. Heat the oil in a wide pan and brown the meat pieces on all sides. Remove from the pan and set aside.

3. Fry the spices in the oil for 2 minutes then add the salt and onion purée and cook for 3 minutes.

4. Return the meat to the pan, add the tomato paste (purée) and lamb broth (stock) then simmer with a lid on very gently for about 45 minutes. Add a little water during the cooking if needed.

5. Add the spinach to the pan and cook for a further 30 minutes or until the lamb is very tender.

INDIAN RICE SALAD

Ingredients

1 cup / 200 g long grain rice

½ cup / 125 ml vegetable oil

4 onions, very finely sliced

2 garlic cloves, chopped

1 tsp salt

1 tsp sugar

2 tsp black onion seeds

8 cardamom pods

8 curry leaves

Salt and pepper

Method

Prep and cook time: 30 min

1. Cook the rice according to packet instructions.

2. While the rice is cooking, heat the oil in a skillet and gently fry the onions and garlic with the salt and sugar, stirring from time to time, until they have started to caramelize and brown – this will take about 15 minutes.

3. Stir in the onion seeds, cardamom pods and curry leaves and cook for 3 more minutes.

4. When the rice is cooked, drain well and rinse then add to the onion mixture. Stir well and season with salt and pepper.

BOMBAY ALOO

Ingredients

6 large potatoes, peeled and cut into chunks

4 tbsp clarified butter or oil

1 onion, finely chopped

1 tsp cumin seeds

2 tsp black onion seeds

1 tsp mustard seeds

1 tsp fenugreek seeds

½ tsp curcuma (turmeric)

1 tsp garam masala

2 red chili peppers, deseeded and chopped

4 curry leaves, roughly chopped

1 cup / 200 g canned tomatoes, chopped

1 tsp salt

Cilantro (fresh coriander), to garnish

Method
Prep and cook time: 40 min

1. Boil the potatoes in a large pan of salted water until tender. Drain well and set aside.

2. Heat the butter in a wide skillet and fry the onion until soft but not brown. Add the all the seeds, curcuma (turmeric), garam masala and chili peppers and cook for 2 more minutes.

3. Stir in the curry leaves then add the tomatoes and salt and simmer very gently for about 15 minutes, stirring from time to time, until the sauce is very thick. Add a little water during the cooking if needed to prevent burning.

4. Stir the potatoes into the sauce and garnish with the cilantro (fresh coriander). Serve with boiled rice.

TIGER SHRIMPS
MAHARAJA STYLE

Ingredients

3 tbsp clarified butter or oil

2 garlic cloves, finely chopped

Thumb-size piece ginger, peeled
and finely chopped

1 red chili pepper, deseeded and
finely chopped

1 tsp garam masala

2 cups / 500 ml coconut milk

1 cup / 250 ml fish broth (stock)
or water

20 tiger shrimps (prawns), peeled with
tails left on

Juice of 1 lime

1 tbsp chopped cilantro
(fresh coriander)

Salt and pepper

Parsley sprigs, to garnish

Method
Prep and cook time: 20 min

1. Heat the butter in a wide pan and gently cook
the garlic, ginger and chili pepper until soft but
not brown.

2. Add the garam masala, cook for 1 minute then
pour in the coconut milk and fish broth (stock) and
simmer gently for about 10 minutes.

3. Add the shrimps (prawns) and simmer for 5 more
minutes or until the shrimps are cooked through. Stir
in the lime juice, season with salt and pepper and
add the chopped cilantro (coriander).

TANDOORI CHICKEN WITH RAITA

Ingredients

For the chicken:

4 chicken breasts, skinned

1 tsp each: garam masala, ground cumin, curcuma (turmeric)

2 tsp paprika

2 red chili peppers, deseeded and finely chopped

4 garlic cloves, finely chopped

1 tbsp tomato paste (purée)

Thumb-size piece fresh ginger, peeled and finely chopped

4 tbsp yogurt

1 tsp salt

Juice of 1 lemon

For the raita:

1 cup / 250 ml yogurt

½ cucumber, seeds removed and finely sliced

2 sprigs mint, leaves finely chopped

1 tsp salt

½ green chili pepper, deseeded and finely chopped

To serve: 4 tomatoes, chopped and flat breads

Method
Prep and cook time: 20 min plus 8 hours to marinate

1. Cut the chicken breasts into wide strips and set aside.

2. Mix the remaining ingredients for the chicken together to make a paste and rub into the chicken slices. Cover and refrigerate for 8 hours.

3. For the raita, mix together all the ingredients and set aside.

4. Heat the broiler (grill) or barbecue to a medium setting. Thread the chicken slices onto wooden skewers and broil (grill) for about 3 minutes on each side or until the chicken is cooked through.

5. Serve the skewers with the raita, chopped tomatoes and flat breads alongside.

CHICKEN KERALA

Ingredients

6 tbsp oil

2 red onions, finely sliced

16 curry leaves

1 white onion, finely chopped

2 garlic cloves, chopped

Thumb-size piece ginger, peeled and finely chopped

1 tsp curcuma (turmeric)

1 tsp garam masala

2 red chili peppers, deseeded and finely chopped

1 tsp mustard seeds, crushed

1 tsp coriander seeds, crushed

4 cloves, crushed

1 tsp peppercorns, crushed

1 tsp salt

4 chicken breasts, skinned and cut into chunks

½ cup / 125 ml chicken broth (stock)

½ cup / 125 ml coconut milk

Method

Prep and cook time: 45 min

1. Heat the oil in a large skillet and gently fry the red onions until crisp but not burnt. Remove from the skillet and set aside.

2. Fry the curry leaves for 2 minutes then set aside.

3. Fry the white onion gently until soft but not brown then add the garlic, ginger, curcuma (turmeric), garam masala, chili peppers, mustard seeds, coriander seeds, cloves, peppercorns and salt.

4. Fry the mixture for 2 minutes then add the chicken. Stir briefly then pour in the chicken broth (stock) and coconut milk. Simmer gently, stirring from time to time, for 20 minutes or until the chicken is cooked through.

5. Serve with the fried red onions scattered over and the curry leaves to garnish.

ONION BHAJIS WITH MANGO CHUTNEY

Ingredients

For the bhajis:

1 tbsp coriander seeds

1 tbsp cumin seeds

1 cup / 75 g gram (chickpea) flour

½ tsp baking powder

1 tsp salt

2 onions, grated

Oil, for frying

For the chutney:

2 tsp coriander seeds

2 tsp cumin seeds

1 tsp black onion seeds

1 cup / 250 ml white wine vinegar

1 cup / 250 g muscovado sugar

1 tsp salt

½ red chili pepper, deseeded and finely chopped

2 mangoes, peeled, stoned removed and cut into chunks

Method

Prep and cook time: 1 hour

1. For the chutney, lightly toast the coriander seeds, cumin seeds and black onion seeds in a hot, dry pan for 30 seconds.

2. Put the vinegar and sugar in a small pan and heat until the sugar has dissolved then add the toasted seeds, the salt and chili and let bubble for 5 minutes then add the mangoes and cook very gently for 20 minutes, stirring from time to time, or until very thick, then set aside.

3. For the bhajis, lightly toast the coriander seeds and cumin seeds in a hot, dry pan.

4. Sift the flour into a bowl and add the toasted seeds, baking powder, salt and grated onions. Add just enough water to make a very thick batter.

5. Heat the oil in a deep pan until bubbles appear on a wooden spoon held in the oil. Drop small balls of the batter into the oil in batches and deep fry for 3–4 minutes or until golden brown. Drain on kitchen paper and serve with the mango chutney.

INDIAN GREEN BEAN SALAD

Ingredients

3 cups / 450 g string (green) beans, cut into small pieces

4 tbsp coconut oil or vegetable oil if unavailable

6 curry leaves

1 tsp mustard seeds

1 tsp fenugreek seeds

1 tsp coriander seeds

1 tsp fennel seeds

2 cloves garlic, finely chopped

2 red chili peppers, split in half

lengthways

3 tbsp lemon juice

¾ cup / 60 g coconut, grated (or desiccated coconut)

Method

Prep and cook time: 30 min

1 Blanch the beans in boiling water for 2 minutes, drain, refresh in cold water and drain once more. Set the beans aside.

2 Heat the oil in a wide skillet and fry the curry leaves for 30 seconds then remove from the pan and set aside.

3 Put the mustard seeds, fenugreek seeds, coriander seeds, and fennel seeds in the pan and cook over a medium heat, stirring all the time, for 2 minutes.

4 Add the garlic and chili peppers, cook for 3 more minutes then stir in the green beans.

5 Add the lemon juice and stir for one more minute. Serve garnished with the curry leaves and the coconut sprinkled over.

DHAL

Ingredients

1½ cups / 300 g red lentils, rinsed

2 bay leaves

1 tsp salt

1 cinnamon stick

3 tbsp clarified butter or oil

1 onion, finely chopped

2 garlic cloves, finely chopped

Thumb-size piece ginger, peeled and grated

2 tsp curcuma (turmeric)

1 tsp ground cumin

½ tsp garam masala

1 tsp chili powder

Juice of 1 lemon

Salt and pepper

1 tbsp chopped cilantro (fresh coriander), plus some to garnish

Poppadums, to serve

Method
Prep and cook time: 30 min

1. Put the lentils, bay leaves, salt and cinnamon stick in pan with 3 cups (750 ml) of water, bring to a boil and simmer for 15 minutes, stirring from time to time, or until the lentils are soft. Add more water if needed to prevent the mixture becoming dry. Discard the bay leaves and cinnamon stick and set aside.

2. Heat the butter in a pan and gently fry the onion until soft but not brown then add the garlic, ginger, curcuma (turmeric), cumin, garam masala and chili powder. Cook for 2 minutes then stir in the cooked lentils.

3. Add the lemon juice, season with salt and pepper and gently cook for 5 more minutes, stirring all the time to prevent burning.

4. Stir in the chopped cilantro (coriander) and serve garnished with the cilantro leaves and the poppadums alongside.

POTATO PAKORAS WITH YOGURT SAUCE

Ingredients

1 lb / 450 g potatoes

1 cup / 75 g gram (chickpea) flour

$1/3$ cup / 50 g cornmeal (polenta)

1 tsp fennel seeds

3 green chili peppers, deseeded and finely chopped

2 tbsp chopped cilantro (fresh coriander) leaves

1 onion, finely chopped

Sunflower oil, for frying

For the yogurt sauce:

1 cup / 250 ml yogurt

1 tsp sugar

1 pinch salt

1 tbsp chopped cilantro (fresh coriander) leaves

1 tbsp chopped mint leaves

Salt and pepper

Method

Prep and cook time: 1 hour 30 min

1. Cook the potatoes in salted water for 30 minutes or until soft and then mash.

2. Mix the gram flour, cornmeal (polenta) and fennel seeds in a bowl. Stir in the chili, cilantro (fresh coriander) and onion. Then add the potatoes and as much water as necessary to form a thick, kneadable dough.

3. Heat the oil in a deep skillet until bubbles appear on a wooden spoon held in the fat.

4. Drop tsp-sized portions of the dough into the oil and fry until golden yellow. Remove from the pan and pat dry on kitchen paper.

5. To make the yogurt sauce, mix all the ingredients together and season to taste. Serve the potato pakoras with the yogurt sauce.

INDIAN MEATBALLS

Ingredients

1 lb / 450 g ground (minced) lamb

2 scallions (spring onions), finely chopped

2 green chili peppers, deseeded and finely chopped

1 tsbp chopped cilantro (coriander) leaves, plus some to garnish

Salt and pepper

5 tbsp oil

2 onions, finely sliced

2 garlic cloves, finely chopped

Thumb-size piece ginger, peeled and grated

2 tsp garam masala

1 tsp coriander seeds, crushed

1 tsp cumin seeds, crushed

1 cup / 200 g canned tomatoes, chopped

Salt and pepper

Couscous, to serve

Method

Prep and cook time: 45 min

1. Mix the lamb with the scallions (spring onions), chili peppers, cilantro (coriander), salt and pepper and shape into meatballs.

2. Heat 3 tbsp of oil in a wide skillet and fry the meatballs until browned all over. Remove from the skillet and set aside.

3. Heat the remaining oil in the skillet and fry the onions until soft but not brown. Add the garlic, ginger, garam masala, coriander, and cumin seeds and fry for 2 minutes.

4. Return the meatballs to the pan and add the tomatoes and about ½ cup (125 ml) of water. Simmer very gently for 20 minutes or until the meatballs are cooked through. Season with salt and pepper.

5. Serve with couscous and garnish with the cilantro (coriander) leaves.

LAMB JALFREZI

Ingredients

1 tsp cumin seeds

1 tsp black mustard seeds

1 tsp fenugreek seeds

2 tsp garam masala

2 tsp chili powder

1 lb 8 oz / 650 g lamb, from the leg; roughly chopped

4 tbsp clarified butter or oil

2 onions, finely sliced into rings

1 green bell pepper, deseeded and sliced

Method

Prep and cook time: 25 min plus 1 h to marinate

1. Mix the cumin seeds, mustard seeds, fenugreek seeds, garam masala and chili powder together and coat the lamb with the mixture. Leave to marinate for at least 1 hour

2. Heat the oil in a wide skillet and fry the onion until soft but not brown.

3. Add the meat and the marinade, fry over a high heat for 5 minutes, stirring all the time, then add the green bell pepper and cook for 3 minutes or until the lamb is cooked through and the peppers are tender. Serve with rice.

CAULIFLOWER CURRY WITH CHICKPEAS

Ingredients

3 tbsp oil

1 onion, finely chopped

2 garlic cloves, chopped

Thumb-size piece of ginger, peeled and grated

1 tsp chili powder

3 tsp garam masala

1 lb / 450 g potatoes, diced

1 lb / 450 g cauliflower florets

1 cup / 250 ml vegetable broth (stock) or water

1 cup / 250 ml yogurt

1½ cups / 300 g canned chickpeas, drained

2 handfuls spinach, washed and roughly chopped

3 tbsp lemon juice

1 tsp paprika

Salt and pepper

Lemon wedges, to garnish

Method

Prep and cook time: 45 min

1. Heat the oil in a large skillet and gently fry the onion until soft but not brown.

2. Add the garlic, ginger, chili powder and garam masala and fry for 2 minutes.

3. Stir in the potatoes and cook gently for 5 minutes. Add the cauliflower, cook for 2 minutes then add the vegetable broth (stock) and yogurt and simmer over a low heat for 15 minutes.

4. Add the chickpeas and spinach and cook for a further 5 minutes then stir in the lemon juice and season with salt and pepper. Serve garnished with lemon wedges and sprinkled with paprika.

LAMB IN SPINACH *SAUCE*

Ingredients

1 cup / 250 ml yogurt

2 tsp ground coriander

1 tsp each: ground cumin, curcuma (turmeric) and chili powder

1 tsp salt

1 lb 8 oz / 650 g lamb, from the leg, cut into chunks

4 tbsp clarified butter or oil

1 onion, finely chopped

2 garlic cloves, chopped

Thumb-size piece ginger, peeled and finely chopped

Juice of 1 lime

2 handfuls spinach, washed and roughly chopped

To serve:

Fresh ginger, peeled and cut into thin matchsticks

1 tsp paprika

Method

Prep and cook time: 1 hour plus 1 hour to marinate

1. Mix the yogurt with the coriander, cumin, curcuma (turmeric), chili powder and salt in a large bowl. Add the lamb and set aside to marinate for 1 hour.

2. Heat the butter in a wide pan and gently fry the onion until soft but not brown. Add the garlic and ginger, cook for 1 minute then add the meat and the marinade.

3. Simmer very gently for 45 minutes or until the meat is tender. Add the lime juice and spinach and cook for a further 5 minutes.

4. Serve with the ginger matchsticks and paprika sprinkled over.

PORK WITH COCONUT AND GINGER SAUCE

Ingredients

5 tbsp vegetable oil

1 lb 8 oz / 650 g pork loin, cut into chunks

1 onion, very finely chopped

2 garlic cloves, finely chopped

Thumb-size piece fresh ginger, peeled and grated

Juice of 2 limes

2 cups / 500 ml coconut milk

Salt and pepper

To serve:

1 tbsp dried red chilies, crumbled

2 thumb-size pieces fresh ginger, peeled and cut into matchsticks

$^2/_3$ cup / 100 g cashew nuts, roughly chopped

Method

Prep and cook time: 35 min

1. Heat 3 tbsp of the oil in a wide skillet and fry the pork pieces for about 8 minutes, stirring from time to time, or until golden brown and cooked through. Remove the meat from the skillet, set aside and keep warm.

2. Meanwhile, heat the remaining oil in the skillet and gently fry the onion until soft but not brown. Add the garlic and ginger and cook for 1 more minute.

3. Sprinkle the lime juice into the skillet along with a splash of water, let it bubble for 1 minute and stir well. Pour in the coconut milk and simmer for about 15 minutes, stirring from time to time, or until the mixture has thickened and reduced by about a half. Season with salt and pepper.

4. To serve, stir the meat into the coconut mixture and place in warmed serving bowls. Sprinkle over the dried chilies, ginger matchsticks and cashew nuts and serve immediately.

HOT AND SOUR LAMB

Ingredients

4 tbsp vegetable oil or ghee

2 onions, very finely chopped

2 garlic cloves, finely chopped

1 red chili, deseeded and finely chopped

1 tsp ground cinnamon

2 tbsp mustard seeds

Thumb-size piece fresh ginger, peeled and grated

1 tsp ground cumin

2 lb 8 oz / 1½ kg lamb, cut into large chunks

2 tomatoes, deseeded and chopped

½ cup / 125 ml white wine vinegar

Salt and pepper

Chopped parsley, to garnish

Method

Prep and cook time: 1 hour 45 min

1. Heat the oil in a large pan and gently cook the onions until soft. Stir in the garlic, chili, cinnamon, mustard seeds, ginger and cumin and cook for 2 more minutes.

2. Turn the heat up and add the lamb. Brown the meat on all sides then add the tomatoes and vinegar and season with salt and pepper. Pour in about 1 cup of water and simmer very gently for about 1¼ hours, stirring frequently, or until the meat is very tender. Add more water if needed during the cooking but bear in mind the finished dish should be fairly dry.

3. Serve with rice and garnished with chopped parsley.

BLACKENED CHICKEN STICKS

Ingredients

For the marinade:

3 tbsp cumin seeds

2 garlic cloves, crushed

Thumb-size piece fresh ginger, peeled and grated

4 tbsp vegetable oil

1 tsp salt

2 tsp garam masala

Juice of half a lemon

½ cup / 125 ml yogurt

½ tsp chili powder

4 chicken breasts, skinned

2 tbsp butter

To serve:

Arugula (rocket), cherry tomatoes and pitta breads

Method

Prep and cook time: 30 min plus 2 hours to marinate

1. Toast the cumin seeds in a dry pan for 2 minutes then crush.

2. Mix the cumin seeds with the garlic, ginger, 2 tbsp of the oil, salt, garam masala, lemon juice, yogurt and chili powder.

3. Put the chicken breasts between two sheets of plastic wrap (clingfilm) and bash with a rolling pan to flatten. Slice into strips, mix the chicken with the marinade and set aside for 2 hours.

4. Heat the butter and the remaining oil in a skillet and fry the chicken strips on all sides, basting with the marinade, until browned and cooked through.

5. Serve with the arugula (rocket), cherry tomatoes and pitta breads

Published by Transatlantic Press

First published in 2011

Transatlantic Press
38 Copthorne Road, Croxley Green, Hertfordshire WD3 4AQ

© Transatlantic Press

Images and Recipes by StockFood © The Food Image Agency

Recipes selected by Jonnie Léger, StockFood

A catalogue record for this book is available from the British Library.

ISBN 978-1-907176-88-3

Printed in China